I0467399

Finding a Niche:

Beginner's Guide to Market Research

Written by Susan Kilmer

Copyright © 2015 Provident Wellness

All Rights Reserved.

© Copyright 2015 by Provident Wellness

All rights reserved.

This document is geared towards providing exact and reliable information in regards to the topic and issue covered. The publication is sold with the idea that the publisher is not required to render accounting, officially permitted, or otherwise, qualified services. If advice is necessary, legal or professional, a practiced individual in the profession should be ordered.

- From a Declaration of Principles which was accepted and approved equally by a Committee of the American Bar Association and a Committee of Publishers and Associations.

In no way is it legal to reproduce, duplicate, or transmit any part of this document in either electronic means or in printed format. Recording of this publication is strictly prohibited and any storage of this document is not allowed unless with written permission from the publisher. All rights reserved.

The information provided herein is stated to be truthful and consistent, in that any liability, in terms of inattention or otherwise, by any usage or abuse of any policies, processes, or directions contained within is the solitary and utter responsibility of the recipient reader. Under no circumstances will any legal responsibility or blame be held against the publisher for any reparation, damages, or monetary loss due to the information herein, either directly or indirectly.

Respective authors own all copyrights not held by the publisher.

The information herein is offered for informational purposes solely, and is universal as so. The presentation of the information is without contract or any type of guarantee assurance.

The trademarks that are used are without any consent, and the publication of the trademark is without permission or backing by the trademark owner. All trademarks and brands within this book are for clarifying purposes only and are the owned by the owners themselves, not affiliated with this document.

Introduction

I wanted to start off for thanking you for taking an interest in this book. The main purpose of ***Finding a Niche: Introduction to Market Research*** is to assist both the aspiring entrepreneur and seasoned business owner alike better understand how to assess the viability of the business they would like to start or ideas they have with adding a new product/service, expansion or growth.

The average individual knows at one time or another that they want to either start a business or grow their business but very few know or take the time to find out if that new idea will do well into an already established market place that existed long before their idea came along.

My goal for this market research guide is for you to understand what market research is, the purpose and benefits, type of information you should want to collect, how to perform market research and how to not only evaluate the data you collect but also how to analyze it to assist you in making the appropriate decisions for your business.

By the time you read the entire book, you will have a better the market research process which is a detrimental part of any business. Market research assists you assess the viability of any decision you make in your business. It's better to be safe than sorry right!?

Enjoy!

Chapter 1

What is Market Research?

The top question every aspiring entrepreneur needs to ask themselves about their business is: ***What problem does it solve or what need does it fulfill?***

There are many reasons why consumers make purchase decisions, but the primary one is **need**. Consumers purchase based on what their immediate needs are but also their immediate needs especially with the type of product or service they want to purchase. It is your job as a business owner to find out what a specific customer's exact needs are related to the type of products and services that your business sells and how you can shape your business to meet their needs. For your business to do well, you will need to sell the product to a customer in the way they want, at the price they want in the locations they want.

Market research can help you clarify this.

Through research you will be able to gather certain information and data such as: **demographics, size of your potential market, customer lifestyles** and **buying behavior,** specifically who the customer is and then determine the demand for your product or service.

Market research is a key part of developing your overall marketing strategy. It is about collecting information to give you an insight into the minds of your customers so that you understand what they need. You can also do market research to get a better idea of market trends and what is happening in the industry your business is in.

The information you will gather and evaluate helps build the core foundation of correct business strategies whether it's deciding what product or service you want to sell, where your business should be located, how to sell your products or how you will communicate with consumers.

Chapter 2

Purpose and Benefits of Market Research

There are many benefits to why a business owner needs to research the market place they would like to enter into or expand into, but there is one main purpose:

Will my business do well in the business environment I would like to enter into?

Unless you are psychic, there is no way for you to tell without research. The more you know about what you are getting into, the better you can develop the appropriate business, products/services, and marketing strategies that will enable you to reach the customers you ideally want to sell to.

After all, whether your potential customers buy from you will determine if you earn enough revenue to keep your business open day-to-day, month-to-month and year-to-year.

Benefits of Market Research:

- Helps you determine overall your business idea's potential

- Helps you define marketing opportunities and problems within your industry

- Helps you better align your products or services with your target market and helps you deliver better to them.

- Helps you develop a strong understanding of how your competitors operate.

- Helps you set realistic targets and develop effective strategies

- Helps you identify industry best practices

- Better awareness of market gaps and pain points

Chapter 3

Information You Need to Collect

Business owners need to know their market, competitors, customers and what it takes to be competitive before they start and while in operation. Essentially at **all** times.

Market research involves asking the questions, taking time to learn about various factors that can impact your business both externally and internally.

Market research also involves watching your customers in order to figure out how they make decisions, are there enough customers to thrive or just survive. Also, who are your competitors – what are their capabilities and weaknesses.

The information you need to collect is:

1) **Industry** – The entire picture of what is happening in the environment of your type of business. Market research will help you become more aware of industry trends, shifts and changes to the economy.

    a. Are there any population shifts?

    b. Are there any legal or regulatory developments?

    c. Growth trends?

    d. Changes in the local economic climate?

    e. Lifestyle changes? (# of single parents, working women, smaller family sizes, etc.)

    f. Etc.

2) **Target Customers** – Marketing your business can help you reach your target market, but first you must know who they are. You will need to identify their demographics and psychographics:

    a. Age

    b. Income Level

    c. Occupation

d. Family Size

e. Marital Status

f. Residence

g. Interests and Hobbies

h. Etc.

3) **Customer Needs and Buying Patterns** – You can also improve your product or service based on findings about what your customers really want and need. Some things you will want to know:

a. Do people like and need your product/service?

b. Will they need it for a limited time or infrequently?

c. How much will they be willing to pay?

d. When deciding who to buy from, what are the key factors?

    i. Is it price, selection, location, turnaround time/order time, service, quality, expertise, reliability, hours, reputation, company size, distribution channels, etc.

4) **Competitors** – To gain better understanding of the strengths and weaknesses of your competition. You need to collect data on factors such as:

    a. How your competition promotes their products

    b. What their price points are

    c. What their customers think about them

    d. Sales volume

    e. What strengths do they promote and advertise, etc.

Chapter 4

Good Research Outcomes

There is a variety of ways to research and it is tough to figure out which direction to head into, especially if you have never performed any type of market research before.

To give you a better sense of the type of information you should have at the end of your research efforts, good research outcomes include:

- Evaluation of potential and current customers

- Who the target customers, what is important to them are and where they are located

- If the product or service your business is selling fit the target customers wants, needs and desires

- How to promote and reach the target customers that want and need the products and/or services that you sell

- Evaluation of current and potential competitors including how they currently sell and what do customers think about them.

Chapter 5

How to Perform Market Research

The first step in the market research process is to <u>define your market research objectives.</u> The scope of your research is determined by what you want to achieve and the types of decisions it needs to help you make. In other words, what is the key information that you would like your research to uncover?

A well written objective is clear, concise, complete and realistic. An objective may be identifying or verifying a target market, identifying or verifying customer needs and wants, finding new opportunities and new markets or estimating the size of markets.

Another objective may be to find out whether people in the community are interested in a certain style of product/service you offer or if they prefer some alternative. Finally, an objective may be to learn whether or not your product or service appeals to the individual's in a specific area.

Once you have identified an objective to investigate, develop a list of research questions to narrow down specifics about your market, customers and competitors such as:

- Is there a demand for my product or service?

- What sales can I expect?

- Who buys my products (i.e. age, gender, income, occupation, and lifestyle)?

- What is the best price for my products or services?

- How should my products look, feel, taste, etc.?

- What is the best location for my business?

- Are other businesses offering similar products or services?

- Is there sufficient demand for my product to make the business viable?

Chapter 6

Where to Research

There are various types of market research – primary, secondary, qualitative and quantitative:

1) **Primary Research** – is research gathered firsthand by collecting data directly from research subjects such as potential customers through techniques like:

   a. **Surveys and Questionnaires**

   b. **Focus Groups**

   c. **Interviews and Polls**

   d. **Product Tests**

   e.

It can be time consuming and/or expensive, however it provides you with the opportunity to hear customer feedback and act accordingly.

Speak with individuals at locations such as trade shows including suppliers, potential customers, even competitors.

Source Examples

- **Target Customers**

  - Customer Surveys

  - Test Marketing

  - Focus Groups

  - Polls

- **Competitors**

  - Website and online search

  - News Articles

  - Social Media

  - Site Visits

  - Telephone Contacts

2) Secondary Research – is already published research that analyzes, compiles or compares existing research data collected by others. It includes sources like:

    a. **Business Directories**

    b. **Industry Journals**

    c. **Industry Reports**

    d. **Newspapers and other forms of media**

    e. **Economic Forecasts**

    f. **Census Data**

    g. **Trade Association Publications**

Secondary research is easily accessible, sometimes less costly and requires less effort and can be conducted on a continual basis. The only disadvantage is it is research you did not conduct yourself and therefore you may not find the exact data you will need.

3) Quantitative Research – is objective data that can include statistical results, financial data and/or demographic data. It includes data such as:

    a. **Total amount consumers spent on a product in a year**

    b. **Past growth rates of an industry**

    c. **Numerical results of consumer surveys**

4) Qualitative Research – is insight and subjective analysis that is expressed in words and not in numbers. It includes sources like:

    a. **Guided group discussion**

    b. **May generate a richer, more complete understanding of participants experiences and benefits**

    c. **Allows a research to dig beyond the surface**

    d. **Experts' observations about what motivators customers**

    e. **Forecasts for future industry trends**

    f. **Subjective comments consumers make about a product**

Source Examples:

- **Industry**

  - American Fact Finder Quick Reports

  - Economic Census

  - Industry Trade Associations

  - ABI/INFORM Global

  - Standard & Poor's Net Advantage

  - Business & Company Resource Center

- **Target Market**

  - US Census Bureau

  - US Census Bureau: International database

  - Sperling's Best Places

  - Mintel

  - MarketResearch.com Academic

- o Stat USA

- **Competitors**

  - o Company Websites

  - o US Securities and Exchange Commission: EDGAR

  - o US Patent and Trademark Office website

  - o Standard & Poor's Net Advantage

  - o Plunkett Research Online

  - o Dun and Bradstreet website

Keep in mind that market research does not necessarily need to be complicated, sophisticated and/or expensive as you decide what answers you are looking for and then decide what the appropriate sources of information you can get those answers from.

For businesses that are currently in operation you can obtain informal data through:

- **Your Employees:** They are your best source of finding out about your customer likes and dislikes since your employees work more directly with customers and hear complaints that may not necessarily make it to the owner. They also become aware of items requested that your business currently may or may not offer.

- **Your Current Customers:** Collecting current customer feedback is an effective form of research. By asking the customers questions such as how items could improve.

- **Current Company Records:** Looking at items such as sales records, complaints, receipts or any other records can indicate what customers currently buy, in what volume and during what time period.

Chapter 7

Potential Research Issues and Evaluation

It is important that you also take the time to identify the issues involved in in your market research. For example:

- **Research Timeline** – Allowing your research deadlines to slip may mean your results occur too late to effectively implement certain decisions and you need to be aware of the time you can afford to invest

- **Research Budget**

- **How you want to use the information**

- **Size** – Data that becomes too large and time consuming may fail to give you the results you need

Understanding issues that could impact on your market research will help you set goals that are realistic and achievable.

Considering issues such as these before you carry out your market research will help ensure you get the information you need without stretching your budget or wasting your time.

Gather, Assess, Adjust and Repeat

Business owners need to take the time to evaluate their findings in order to make decisions about starting the business they would like to start or expanding their business. If research performed properly, business owners should have the information they need to make a GO or NO GO decision about moving forward.

Ask yourself:

- Given what research is revealed, is this the right target? Product? Service?

- Do we need to adjust our target?

- Do we need to change our competitive strategy?

- Are we welling in the right locations?

- Do we need to change our competitive strategy?

- Are we selling in the right locations?

- Do we have a marketing message that appeals to our target market?

- If we make changes, do we need to look at a different group of competitors or factors?

Chapter 8

Sample Data Sites and Take Away

Outside of the sources for market research mentioned throughout this book, there are some additional sources of information that can be handed depending on what your research objectives and questions are:

SBA Size up: www.sizeup.com

This is data on competitors, local industry level data, and buyers/seller

Census: www.census.gov

This is data on US population and economy

Google Trends: www.google.com/trends

This is data on trends in search engine keywords

Go-Biz CalGold: http://calgold.ca.gov

This is permit information for your business, contact information for the various agencies that administer and issue these permits by industry and location.

If there any ideas that you want to create for your business, whether it is to start a business, add a new product/service, expand to a new location or take your business to the next level – market research can help you make decisions on whether the idea is viable depending on the data you find.

If you are starting a business it is important that you find out more information about what your potential customers want, the proper location to sell your products or services, who your competitors are and what are the proper prices to charge your customers.

If you are currently in business and want to expand or grow your business you will need to look into the industry and market trends and also the opinions of your current customers to see if what your plans are will hinder your current business progress or improve on it.

Start to perform preliminary market research on industry, target market and competitors.

REMEMBER:

- What types of information do we need to know?

- How are you going to gather the data?

- Utilizing sources such as: surveys, focus groups, internet research

www.ingramcontent.com/pod-product-compliance
Lightning Source LLC
Chambersburg PA
CBHW081415170526
45166CB00010B/3353